City West

Also by Catherine Walsh:

Making Tents
Short Stories
Pitch
Idir Eatortha

Catherine Walsh

City West

Shearsman Books
Exeter

First published in the United Kingdom in 2005 by
Shearsman Books Ltd.,
58 Velwell Road,
Exeter EX4 4LD

http://www.shearsman.com/

Distributed in the Republic of Ireland by hardPressed Poetry
hpp@gofree.indigo.ie

ISBN 0-907562-54-X

Cover design by the author.
Photograph of the author by Billy Mills.

Acknowledgements

Parts of *City West*, in earlier versions, have been published in *Etruscan Reader 1*
(etruscan books), *Assembling Alternatives* (ed. Romana Huk, Wesleyan University
Press), a chapbook from Longhouse, and in the following magazines:
Boundary 2, The Journal, Boxkite, Talisman and *Big Allis*.

The publisher gratefully acknowledges financial assistance from
Arts Council England.

City West

CITY

— the physical quality of life, that's
living, and not the analysis
afterwards or the moments of
discord or premonition —

there is
    a
    clearer   in a
light   clearer

                            light

            stark   stark
    boles   boles
              bark   bark
  lifting   lifting
                      layer
    layer
    of   experience
      defence
      the curved   curving

                     circumference
   circumference
                    V's
   of V's

branches
white slated road
clothesline spun pipe
left back flawbracket
flood   beneath

                once   (lotteria
starting
building up
            fact card

for   [only]   finding

            application
    wanting   keeping

            safe
not intending   going towards
                        binding
    contracts
                            creating
using
best endeavours
            ensuring
displaying   being better
storing   being directed
            being only

grasp rattle roll

wheeze last
cough
wheeze today
activity

          bramble

if having   query   [concern]

regarding   %

    delicious!

reserving
    open

     now
enclosing   lately likely to

  seed

old bloom spreading   back wall
   next door's gloves secateurs
not cut back   all

   day long   early thirst
night time hunger   among
 between eventing   rotating
          spin
       winging
          by

   one
       day
    long
          tight
    breath   pushing   when
    light
        pull   lifting
              light lifting
    roll

cold blown rose is a

the curiously unformulated

approaching
              ties

copying formulaic patterns

    divide

       thought sectioned
as sanctioned

    religion?
this?

what passes

my mistake
thought

       comical towers

long calls out
    prehensile soundings

a little today!
yes. for me. overdue. she says.
well. waiting. wanting.
getting.

about
        being
natural
            attitude consistently   bidding

        freedoms

            papering   painting buying
                    no necessities   dressing
more all

                a blue-arsed fly
            after
people   conglomerating
                            material
    items   foisting on   categories
            associated

anyone   where's capaciousness?
    distraction
    seconds

    * me   ~   * me   ~   * me   ~

    strangulating
            tying avidly
    over   any citizen

heart
where?
readying   steadying giving taking
loving making breaking coming in going out
spending whiling listening playing
tuning tiptoeing crossing   shh sleeping

knowing they're knowing nothing

enjoying this
prolonged ride
on the current   breezy day

sunlight   blading   floors

[over the road
(she's saying she can't go
home sitting
radio

(going   pram to shops

(home

[radio

rosehips wilden
    April
 holding heat
cornering
   warm
       breeze
         (haze)
                  white   plastic
                   hexagonal
                  nailing gnarled
                  overgrown
 doesn't like   rosebushes
                      wall
    barbarous
                constant
lower overhanging branches
dooming footballs

resting
sweeping brush
   sky
getting   out

   short cricket bat
   clubs all
     broken

5
        1   2   3
chanting
  singing
  baby   listening dancing
clapping   (
  stamping   tapping
sliding   running   circling
  wide
  watching   rounding
  rectilinear
      space
  home   inside

flopping gasping catching
  choosing   reading
raising   lowering   speeding
  slowing   emphasising   relaxing
       story
   remembering   reading
    enjoying
      surprise

                    wilden
              wall holding
          heat
              cornering
                  warmth

        sugar
    leaves

            run thumb
          along smaller
            spines detaching
          minute leaves / holding
           in sleeves / gathering
          plenty   sugar
            house bush

    having been used to sitting a room when
    mine yellow blind up reading the window filled in
    canal cider parties teenage couplings dogs nicked
    cars smashing bollards chain junkies
    glowering light   reading
                    walking
                    looking

        part of   was from part
of there   where

(ain't afraid of the nothin' man
    "   "   at all

    etc.
ain't afraid of the nothin' man
    —comes from nowhere

    and on
        that

teenage song   rang late   pedalling how
do they remain upright at red lights?

    here   now   actually present
doing seeing hearing sometimes
    even understanding breathing days

    longer   shorter   light going on till
    half past   10 or so   brighter nights
        walking home midnight through / over the
Islandbridge gate
    cycling Sandymount   breezed
    face   (miscellaneous wingéd insects
            attached   eyes streaming

is it time?   (what time?
(what's time?)   why?

when? eemph! and anyway, *is* it time

enumerate
dreaded elements?   do I mean?

what's the point?
dashing gerund

should?   ought one   be seen to?
so on   ad infinitum   god it's
boring!   the problem then

again   this is not as
little as it
is now
seeming to be   it's being in doing and in
doing   while
duration   it is being in
span

a certain manner   a series of sequence
same

topping
coat   superficial moving side
 show   overall

    chore
         doing   to

   doing more
dressing up losing
 tempers   going out now

again   movers   perhaps
          convoluted
involvement   locale gender

groups   massive   heavily sign

posted
labelled
 bid

   outside

 / can't see
     / any

   peasouper

.

this currently
listening human
interest social
realism   genders   ages
mix   houses vans   streetsides
halting sites   babies tots
lot factories closing   not opening
never having been built   thought
offered

'the time now is eleven o'clock'
     they've got news   probably can't
bear it   am I?
how?   not listening?   not?
only small a part of myself

atomistic method
  elaborate   structural atomism

     careful selection   devices
        presentation   naming linking
   describing

'for a brand new single from the Corrs'

they say

calendars tell
turning showing
register

    what's the point
not forgotten

     gardens drying clothing
children playing what's that?
running splashing chatting shooting
baskets arguing hacking soft ball round
  squared out shape scooting
  chasing shouting spilling laughing
  laughing

  heads thrown back
    hooting it
I like this kind of tired

           putting off taking
up piece writing another
recently back of
fearing interruption
during which
anticipation going
in out around through how
do?

isolating element (
hit by tennis balls
separate   factor only
perceived as checking
oppositionals sharing
particulars   moot

      interstices

  long lines heavy highlighted
one other one

     could directional symbols
              ?   !
several overs
meanly gravely solemnly
X amount of
saving whatsit for where   school
exercising   over agonising labour counting
glossaries

     word

           all for each
       embodying
         no more significance
other   (   )   itself

                              now go
upstairs brush] your face wash
your hair] teeth   coming down
ready $5^{1}/_{2}$

acting pretty don't
think cook process
product amongst few
firmly embedded   (snort)
(snorting) (what?)   it is
from   all   for
veneration   reverential
lick
             meanwhile

as engaging all these
activities mind hand brain eye
ear foot stomach bowel etc. son's
buttercup garden's coming on
a revival   over   flattened
squashed circumference
small inflatable island
swamped   propped
drying?   lifting?   sticking?
I don't know

too
knowing not
doing sensation
possession knowing's
not needing recognition
frameworks scaffolding
particulars context
circumscribed

static unreal knowing
another memory linking
experiencing dreaming no
knowing knowing knowing

slow repetitious advice crystal
radio sets hams cavity bricks foreign
insects 'phones off hook faulty digital
clocks cheap transistors relative quantities
of silicon pre 1940's building
materials neighbours' domestic animals

      checklist?
10m radius using baby
domestic intercom mobile 'phones
same medium wave popular
station   seasonal allergies
inflammation sound distortion
dental fillings metal body plates

   elemental terror
   they don't know can't control
   self-importance

         air light water
 oxygen nitrogen carbons various
elements

  composite

having no control

voices emanating
erroneous
terror   partitioned terraces

just got tired writing
songs about

certainly people got tired
listening
now   transferring
to   sorted, turned,
pockets emptied
long gap usual
varieties   performed
return folding   baby's awoken

going again

returning perhaps not
pollen count particularly
attractive garden

[pummelled sleeping Niall's head burrowing]

all un / reasonable humans
engaging social activities
common amongst species

watching helicopters circling
small estates sprawling
Dublin flickering

        (damaged
not forgotten

no
   more
than
   breathing
        2
   us
   reality
      running still

a way
thought
      splendid
skimmings
   finely
         whirring
   skin
      while of
   us moving
            out
               only
            bowing
            keeling   may
      never
      close
            .

                    jointed legs
        misbent toes   myopic seers
undarned

whorls
        calling many common images into play

        bridges
            pitches
doing
        what

        stomachs make real

    narrow ironclad causeway
dart arch
    merchant's town

[cycling on through amalgamations
    disintegration's frightening rapidity
    polarised aims

tonight
  many

   night
many more
  even   response to
      from

   unexpected light

   body mind   enduring

    incomprehensible

through out   quotidian

TANGENCY

this aspect tributary oh
free remission hovering air
waves stilling hiccup

relieving springing the hand
on the heavy cracking
   shoulder

manning point butts in heel
hand
ferocious

torpor   written angrily
recurring similitudes widely
 lives

way encountering done after before

[tonal aspect flinging familiar
         syndrome
                        (freaked out
succumbed   ineffable limits   I want
a sandwich phenomenon   what
 (is)   displaced   wind one either

  sending out nationwide
  appeal query
  discrepancy relates

        the figures

retorting
        can be   6 hours   most names having
        some cause]   sounding

hanging on string from a nail I should
slice

    damp penetrating shining the swaying
rosehips readjusting sleeping children attaining
comfort on the green grass icily slushed trunks
corner of shadow gasps to lessen
   does that mean there are 2
separate   unknown   abroad

wide sweeps housing on roads leading round
housing cul de sacs closing encircling roads
one or two towards motorway main
roads roads bearing incessant
weight

    lets face it they're hard at it carving
the rigid chin of the composite capital propping
the bleating (pleated) pilaster

particularising to the point jot

after all assuming affability   the more sets the
more suppositions the more equations the more
terms the more . . .

problem thinking
knowledge

due process leading circulatory
thought deemed consequential

knowledge
grinding halt

should one place be better to stop
than another

always
definitively

or stop as pause   ?

at all?

why should stopping
not involve another part
 of due process

 say decentralisation
at that point (1st grinding halt)
   followed by ... another
    formulaic supposition
                              surely

such supports
would pertain just as
easily

                        jot where

it becomes meaningless

but tight
 tight oh so good and
tight

look!   I start   I exist I
finish!   sincere logical law-abiding

no one part any the less than the
sum of all my parts

(again

          [release   bow
            step back

tropistic behaviour

dialectic-infinite   the ultimate
eluding categories   exhaustion
  deadly!   of
    life   available

      ready with sounds of
            water
and as to why I am

apparently in this position
 the stairs are wooden

getting rid of all
    h

 the literature of he quoted Democritus
sublime caricature Dorothy noted such
shawlies trailing the lonely
evident dearth   stigma

      sending out nationwide querying appeal
a discrepancy the figures   retorting can be up
to 6 hours most names having some cause
sounding the sick hounded   hassled hurt
sometimes killed   not that all are though
it seems a general ruling exists   over a $1/3$ given
wrong

    and traffic

mmmm   I'll tell you what

swish   swish
   up   back   get that

baby in cot from nap in
morning

mother hearing sirens   get that   swish
swish   yes here's your bear
   curtain's open   putting clothes away

putting clothes away   pack'em up pack'em
all away I never want to see'em again

not I
not one
       bit   rose
hips   waving
          by
   speckled bird on
berry bush   bright wall
eyes see   gnarled mushroom
basket red basin cellular growth
within rain filling rain falling
cells in

oh see through trees Irish
critic coming towards   back of sideways
irately most unlike   and so   too

breath
        unconsidered
more
            no sign
    of
expansion

applying elemental forces
        in the crucible   =>

(then you need windows)

    nothing to view
here

tiresome
involvement

  activities than strictly necessary

    further exacerbating traffic
    bumper chaos bumper

    what else could be done?

    delineating   what takes
        up   space

look see recognise name
tell listen retell repeat
all these many times varying order
unchanging landscape
rock beneath

transient   sure   following ways
transferring   names   in recognition
of similarity   difference   aware
extant
threads on terrain   silence

if   hearing   how air
  moving   through
     porous
soil

between rock
        what
      movement
how

many   miniscule
shapes
shifting   patterning so

light, dark   textures
  minute
     particles
affecting   making

shapes   material
  living
matter

  [these are all things that anybody can
  apply without having to go to any
  specialist]

flossy past light stop by hind retreating wreaking
daylight every point stop hugely now light stop so
fine regarding seeking daylight a very pointed
stop justly soon light stop on time depending
meeting daylight early pointers stop lately
will light stop our mind appending leaking
daylight many points stop only if light stop
inside attending reaching daylight lining
point stop

             ah it's this interleaving
                    folding
                    weaving

POW

        consumption in adds monitor cup
        as with is through his school
        is to in of doors wet back
        12.15 p.m. music cars by

what would you like to do?
can you use this axle
these shapes to build?

working in the morning at the round table

imagine[
] change[
          ] imagine
] change[

i   i   more
ing

movements quiet watching

          occasional
          mornings

          light

                    simple
          things

          doing   (
                    hear
[the handcart]

          long shadows incline
          clarity exemplified
          in how not
          achieved not cluster
          natural occurrences
          to the picturesque

          cockadoodledo

          colonising being it
          is still a verb
          important

can't

[
?   was
breathing before

remembering in
the context of the
context remembering

  points   spans

        absence

        always
  shifting   moving on
going
over

missing
the point of missing the
point of missing
the point   is not repetitive

undressed

arresting thought forensic
pile   glitter far out
on ocean   migrating
dissolution removal   resolution
placement   sensational fare
on   ah here get off of that
arrested   thought   frantic
pine   bitter forgotten
  what

                your light houses
                shine   across   kitchens
                we move through

    surely it must reach a point where
    forgetting one
    interior

those   a part
    mentioning   of a   continent
  swifts   told
quick cries   light
  told
  light
        limit less   opening
          succession   shutter
      dazzled   suspending
                   matter
  rock   great
        by   sun

         [solemnly]
    beach and

     (displacement   unheard
              harmonic
              intervals
  stead   unabstracted
    shafts   scale
columns   mathematical proportions
    dense   logic   predicates
      air
       but   leap

        then

                    having attempted
          accretion of
                         to spell
               caesurae
                              out
       listening   to
         many
                              inherent
          symptoms
                     danger
                              music
heart
              less
                         than
                         now
and thinking you've   been

ah well in a letter
                    writing beyond
unable
              notional mausoleum
              studio

          all put
       upon   you can't collect
your   institutes
              though throes   without

there's never enough   to be found

originals in use   being gradually
released from position

though English is spoken here

[derisive cadencing runs through 7 step weave

 (don't live there now either

that's not true / having only seen it happen once

[cyclical intent of monotonous   air

 there   you are   brief spot

less
        lot

  thinking

letters

     might   words pal

  huh   they are

[with care   analytical assurance

                of all
                        relevant precedents
respecting   form   structure   context
usage

                    employed
                    feebly

in lieu   proxy deployment
rolling over on top of your stretched
back wide-mouthed fine thighs whitening
smooth

having all the numbers
 well, enough
    20%   you chance
 upon

    absconding

haven't you?

                        the job of usher

island
in the beam
            pointing out
        moving back

leaving
                    knowing more or less

PLANE

                              watching some one walking a
way down the road buggy pushing
along walking some one a
way down the road buggy pushing
along some one walking a way
down the road buggy pushing along
some one watching some one walking a
way down the road buggy pushing along

—with these problems in mind
this book was initiated—

              At this stage

possession   was everything

              no regard
                   to   gathering   historical
         information

[who called me by my name

   this practice   still
        early   C20th

                              sources
or recognition of any bias in reading contextualising

[and someone

sharp rocks atlantic seas the
breaking out grey Dingle pony white
bay foam still face over lights
coming downhill threaded city into
once again grey walls water sounding
so ambient before through dark
blue brewery harsh vibrant Eccle's
flinty walls St. Catherine's
Bakery, backwards Patriot on
top of the hill narrow wend banks
benches   lock tops   gates   tower blocks
Georgiana bell-on- bell pub-by-pub adjusting
   realigning   points to freeze / decay

   Robert Emmet hanged there
      start   on the way to the jeans shop

what was she looking for?
evidence of some subcultural iconography   or?
evident proof (if found) of supposed deviance
well
stuff it   it's any old
ornament

who do you think you're codding?

that wan
and the dramatic effect

the sign on the
house the
red light burning
   non

stop

                   right
                    lower landing
              gleamings near
                child's cot

   so   told you

waste above all one

                scape
             varying
                   according

most recent
treatment

                                      preventative
        level   measures
           of
                          lack of

white still long pony head easy turning
hair straggling wind abrupt tail

                    pitch
                        dark

dynamo
  picking out spherical moulds
        glimmerings
  lower
                    bay
    bottom
                    steep
      climb

blind
        home

lorry lights road below sea spray all over
mulling a tin dressed in oilskins
again

    yellow and
    blue
                    yellow
relentless turn
mind
            phrasing the
                    best
      part
of
over

                        coercion
                            [+ which machine

that it be seen to start to occur again
regardless of mistrust neglect stupidity

       mistake

usual line   nothing ever happening   false
steps   acknowledgement

        admitting
            appearing

less
     important

            despite

to spite
  unnatural?

   division   mutates   news   exchange

[view
[morning
       oh   morgan says it's so hot
that my garden is drying up
out by roundabouts   swing swong
pools floating sodden woodchips
end of every slide

the time I really thought I was writing
'a book' that got to me more than any of the
knowing full well who knows I thought
       cant
     recant

do try not to pun actually   had a lot of
intentions   none and none at all

for your

      can any one wave goodbye how ever
obliquely   go out a far a distant place a lone for
a long time return 'unspoilt . . . . .

    fine sentiments   they   (?
    however ill
        understood
  interpreted
              a proprietorial
               inclination

expectancy
       validity
        or not of   =

     reflections
   pathos

one of many extraneous details unfortunately
not inconsequential
every time I come to that part of the
story tongue slips stumbling through I
finish the line up on boo
        Jezus – who *writes* these books?

the face of anyone
selecting   highlights

                active clause

  askance

eyes askance
               part time effect living with
  inhibitions
  reticence
        mythical castles
     doors shut worst
     own
     ones

   plain straight

   always another language

the city
  inhabited
these memories   mine   moves

studded   stations   backwards

back and forth actually
        cellular cohesion   .

                      intricate   lore
                            sprawls
        slates   tiles   rocky
            hills   ragged
        edges   round the blanket
        of smog

                  now dusted softly   see
                                                        on the
        and cloudscapes   the   bridge
        communicating   from
            forevers further   the
                                                        square

        patternless   and beautiful

            shudders

                winds   pacts and divides
                    old place names
                  deepening the grooves
gullies
echoing the
unforgotten ones
the first landed
the founders
        anarchy of the flesh

    white lights
  turning up the mountains
white light   rails parks
    white light
            necessity   the
          endeavouring   sane

among realities care about realities you
could   imagine   more

      the festivities of the saint
  long noisy violent
  bank holiday weekends
  dreary   premonition
            unpredictable
  combustions
  spark unknown
city *wants*

             night accommodates all
    cries   children   swinging
          trees   street shattering
glass   glass the vein pricks
stand naked with their
clothes on uniformly faceless
   advertising their
skill motionless flickering
eyes   then the yahoo
the dart   wrestling

         thudding feet
hammering down the road
   by   shouts or screams
stop it stop it fuck off you

putting the children
   back to sleep   closing
a window or 2 despite
heat
               are the jeans still
on the clothesline   who's
had the trainers pulled off
their

it was very dark

hey you how woz?

yo!   hi ya   wanna
ha've

ho,   ho yeah
he?   he,   he wanna be her

how 'ye?   a yeah rih

yo!   geh da wan   ha ha

hey hey   heya   hiya   hi

wanna ha'veh   laugh

geh lahst   ingohin' in

in the very beginning
   night oppressed
                    impenetrable
   ever from the beginning

to fruit   bursting through the sod

            these gods are like this

there we go
        tracing   lines

            little excursive ploys
       the curved plane

who doesn't
        gain sake
forsooth   [goodness sake
doors swinging
                [clap
leap]
        don't jump back

  well maybe we could
  tell you a story
  of the same name

        tendentious
                inexorably
eschewed
acceptance   than life

twisted by imperfect intellects into artificial forms

that   time
   strain   great
                                         exhaustion
love
                         vibrating
                         expanse

                                              indeed inhabiting
      same space   air
                                         breathing light
      as sound   vice versa
                              (viscera   I
      opaque
                         chrysallis
sallies

         clarifying]   nothing

[yes

      sigh   light   displacement of what
      air   humidity   infinitesmal
      minute   particles   mites

  fractal   on the plane or
    shift in perception
peripheral   inclusion
     visuals   matter?
or periphery   including
  the subsequential
mathematical   series
   adjusting   notional perceptions of
how light travels?

cat by left shoulder   walking
dog on wall right

    god to some   or steak

hovering   inexplicable   quality

  sensation

      achieved

       then there's deja vu and petit mal

                    defiant
                                    bare
                    magnolia   peels
away   the middle march
the tattoo

                                    colour
                                    predominating
                    sounding
                                            clear
                    clef to

                                    hearing
[moments snatched taken

[back

                    movements sedimented dispersal

still colour questioning discourse
text animation lighting dialogue

(bodies in darkness)

upreared one
cat
terrible one
fat face
turned face
the one belonging to cobra

salutations

the cat
the gory one
the swallower of millions

from the the
from the the from the the from
the the from the the

    fruitful
feeble   night

    sun up
        hard true centre
          of dawn

splinter stone

shadows   cross
water   stick
   edges arrow
         down
shore?

country plain
these 'angels' euphemisms
engrained theodoxy
     another
wind freezes
      crags
stumps
         hollows
    nothing leaves
emerges

[owned]

wind glides   desolate
            stretching out prone

calm
        nothing
                pondered
existed
sound thread
                breath

sudden incursion of
      magical substance
(from?)

stamped upon it repeatedly

the picture
      will
      show

name nowhere
excavated
broken off

to be seen
in the clear   transparent air

to be seen
to contend with ones face

worked
shatter grind

there are asperous places
        dark/light

abyss

it is
  ashen

sings
      falls out on the
shore
      grey
spiralled
          resounding marvelous
      head

                    centre

satisfying

                        tender verdant

required
precipitous
crumbling

wild horse black road star
strong white eyes water courage
firm pith fire high dry trunk
path stores it signifies among

from the the from the the from the the
the of the

great spread out

day blaze
                    sky

seacht n-amhrán déag is trí scór
léiriú atá I gcuid de scéalta seo ar
an teannas idir an seandearcadh
dúchasach agus an meon nua-aoiseach,
nua- aimseartha
suite san am í láthair, san am atá
caite, agus san am atá le teacht atá
an sceal seo
cén deireadh a bheidh leis?

seventy seven songs
many of these stories focus on the
tension between traditional native ideas
of the world and more modern ways of
looking at things
a story that unfolds in the past, in
the present and in the future
where will it all end?

but with the picture in mind
which I have often thought
counting inadequate resources
looking at the map, the details, whatever,
emerged, without prompting,
in a natural way
(prior)
— to think of your public rather than of
the truth of what you say is, for
instance, quite common and not
regarded as a crime —

(we liked your story so
  much

            eem ah
           amm   eh
           oh   yes

            had a lot of fun
but it's time
to go

(that's very warm

                because
                my favourite game
                is

                    (time to go)

www.ingramcontent.com/pod-product-compliance
Lightning Source LLC
Chambersburg PA
CBHW031929080426
42734CB00007B/617